NFL TODAY

THE STORY OF THE

CINCINNATI BENGALS

D1638338

NFL TODAY

THE STORY OF THE CINCINNATI BENGALS

SARA GILBERT

CREATIVE EDUCATION • CREATIVE PAPERBACKS

PUBLISHED BY CREATIVE EDUCATION AND CREATIVE PAPERBACKS
P.O. BOX 227, MANKATO, MINNESOTA 56002
CREATIVE EDUCATION AND CREATIVE PAPERBACKS ARE
IMPRINTS OF THE CREATIVE COMPANY
WWW.THECREATIVECOMPANY.US

DESIGN AND PRODUCTION BY BLUE DESIGN
ART DIRECTION BY RITA MARSHALL
PRINTED IN THE UNITED STATES OF AMERICA

PHOTOGRAPHS BY CORBIS (MICHAEL KEATING/AP),
GETTY IMAGES (SYLVIA ALLEN/NFL, TYLER BARRICK,
SCOTT BOEHM, CLIFTON BOUTELLE/NFL, PETER
BROUILLET/NFL, KEVIN C. COX, DIAMOND IMAGES,
NED DISHMAN, DAVID DRAPKIN, GIN ELLIS, ELSA, GREG
FIUME, GEORGE GOJKOVICH, SAM GREENWOOD, OTTO
GREULE/ALLSPORT, SCOTT HALLERAN/ALLSPORT,
TOM HAUCK, ANDY LYONS, AL MESSERSCHMIDT,
DONALD MIRALLE, NFL, PETER PEARSON, JOE
ROBBINS, GEORGE ROSE, MANNY RUBIO/NFL, DILIP
VISHWANAT, HARRY E. WALKER/MCT)

LIBRARY OF CONGRESS CATALOGING-IN-PUBLICATION DATA
GILBERT, SARA.
THE STORY OF THE CINCINNATI BENGALS / SARA GILBERT.
P. CM. — (NFL TODAY)
INCLUDES INDEX.
SUMMARY: THE HISTORY OF THE NATIONAL FOOTBALL LEAGUE'S
CINCINNATI BENGALS, SURVEYING THE FRANCHISE'S BIGGEST
STARS AND MOST MEMORABLE MOMENTS FROM ITS INAUGURAL
SEASON IN 1968 TO TODAY.
ISBN 978-1-60818-298-5 (HARDCOVER)
ISBN 978-0-89812-851-2 (PBK)
1. CINCINNATI BENGALS (FOOTBALL TEAM)—HISTORY—JUVENILE
LITERATURE. I. TITLE.

GV956.C6G554 2013
796.332'640977178—DC23   2012028440

HC 9 8 7 6 5 4 3 2 1
PBK 9 8 7 6 5 4 3 2

COVER: QUARTERBACK ANDY DALTON
PAGE 2: RUNNING BACK BENJARVUS GREEN-ELLIS
PAGES 4–5: RUNNING BACK PETE JOHNSON
PAGE 6: WIDE RECEIVER A. J. GREEN

TABLE OF CONTENTS

SIDELINE STORIES

MEET THE BENGALS

IN SPORTS, CINCINNATI EARNED GREATEST FAME FOR ITS BASEBALL REDS

Building the Bengals

When Cincinnati, Ohio, was founded in 1788, it was known as Losantiville, a name put together with words from several languages to describe its location on the Ohio River. It was given its current name in 1790, but since then it has been known by a number of different nicknames as well. In the early 1800s, when Cincinnati was the country's hub for pork processing, the packs of pigs running through the streets led to its being called "Porkopolis." It was also dubbed "The Queen City of the West" after poet Henry Wadsworth Longfellow wrote about the city in 1854. Today, many residents still proudly call Cincinnati the "Queen City."

The other nicknames that matter most in Cincinnati belong to the city's professional sports teams. The Reds have played baseball in Cincinnati since 1869, making them the oldest professional baseball team still in existence. And football teams known as the Bengals have made the city home at least twice, including the Bengals that now represent southwestern Ohio in the National Football League (NFL).

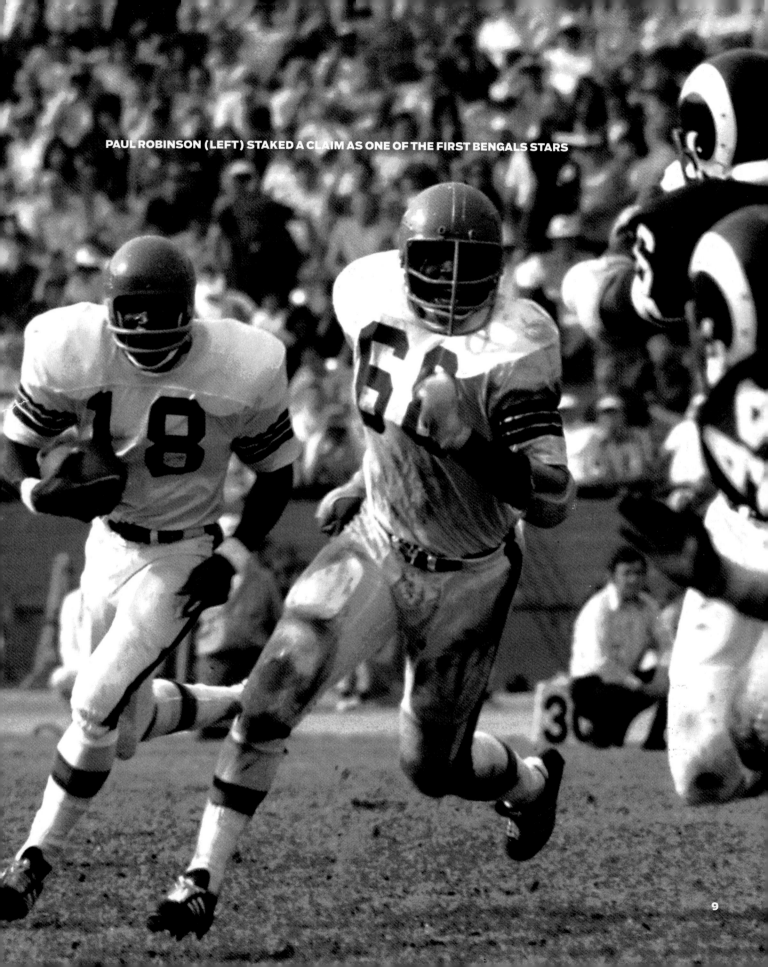

PAUL ROBINSON (LEFT) STAKED A CLAIM AS ONE OF THE FIRST BENGALS STARS

Paul Brown

COACH, TEAM OWNER / BENGALS SEASONS: 1968–75 (AS COACH); 1968–91 (AS OWNER/PRESIDENT)

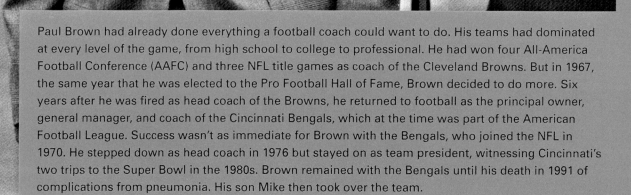

Paul Brown had already done everything a football coach could want to do. His teams had dominated at every level of the game, from high school to college to professional. He had won four All-America Football Conference (AAFC) and three NFL title games as coach of the Cleveland Browns. But in 1967, the same year that he was elected to the Pro Football Hall of Fame, Brown decided to do more. Six years after he was fired as head coach of the Browns, he returned to football as the principal owner, general manager, and coach of the Cincinnati Bengals, which at the time was part of the American Football League. Success wasn't as immediate for Brown with the Bengals, who joined the NFL in 1970. He stepped down as head coach in 1976 but stayed on as team president, witnessing Cincinnati's two trips to the Super Bowl in the 1980s. Brown remained with the Bengals until his death in 1991 of complications from pneumonia. His son Mike then took over the team.

The Bengals started out in 1968 as part of the new American Football League (AFL), which was launched as a rival to the NFL. Paul Brown, the team's owner, general manager, and coach, filled his first roster with a combination of castoff veteran players and unproven rookies. One of those rookies, running back Paul Robinson, scored Cincinnati's first touchdown by running two yards into the end zone in the season opener that year. Robinson's 1,023 yards and 9 touchdowns—feats worthy of the AFL's Rookie of the Year honors—were the bright spots in an otherwise disappointing 3–11 season.

Cincinnati's 1969 effort ended in similar fashion, but in 1970, as the AFL merged with the NFL, the Bengals improved to an 8–6 record, earning the American Football Conference (AFC) Central Division title and making their first trip to the playoffs. Although they lost in the first round to the eventual Super Bowl champion Baltimore Colts, the Bengals had tasted success and were eager to experience more of it.

Three years later, with young quarterback Ken Anderson under center, speedy Essex Johnson running the ball, and sure-handed rookie Isaac Curtis streaking across the field, they got another chance. The talented Bengals got Cincinnati sports fans buzzing by winning 10 games and returning to the playoffs.

"Everybody in Cincinnati is proud of you."

FORREST GREGG ON
SUPER BOWL XVI

This time, it was the Miami Dolphins who eliminated Cincinnati in the first round.

Anderson developed into one of the finest passers in football, finding favorite targets such as Curtis and tight end Bob Trumpy so frequently that he earned the first of his four trips to the Pro Bowl during the 1975 season. Cincinnati put together an impressive 11–3 record that year and made its third appearance in the playoffs. But once again, it lost in the first round. Just days after that defeat, Coach Brown announced that he was stepping down from coaching so that he could concentrate on being general manager. He turned his on-field duties over to Bill Johnson, who had been an assistant coach since the team's beginning.

Anderson remained one of the best quarterbacks in the league, and bruising fullback Pete Johnson strengthened the Bengals' running game, but Cincinnati couldn't get back to the playoffs until 1981. Then, as they introduced their distinctively tiger-striped uniforms and helmets, the Bengals roared back into contention with a 12–4 record. Linebacker Reggie Williams led a stingy defense, receiver Cris Collinsworth brought energy to the offense, and Anderson set new team records for passing yards (3,754) and touchdown passes (29) in a season. The Bengals won their division and readied themselves for the postseason stage.

This time, the Bengals, led by head coach Forrest Gregg, toppled their first-round opponents, the Buffalo Bills, 28–21 to advance to the AFC Championship Game. When the Bengals won a lopsided match against the San Diego Chargers, they found themselves headed to the Super Bowl.

At halftime of Super Bowl XVI, the Bengals trailed the San Francisco 49ers 20–0. In an amazing second-half comeback, Cincinnati scored 21 points. But a pair of San Francisco field goals put the game out of reach; when the clock expired, Cincinnati had lost, 26–21. After the game, Coach Gregg reassured his disappointed players. "You guys played one heck of a second half," he told them. "Everybody in Cincinnati is proud of you, and you should take pride in yourselves."

Although an NFL players' strike shortened the 1982 season, the Bengals' 7–2 record was good enough to send them to the playoffs again, where the New York Jets quickly eliminated them. Then the offense sputtered, and the 1983 season started with six losses in the first seven weeks. Gregg resigned

The Original Bengals

When Paul Brown brought professional football back to Cincinnati in 1968 after a 26-year absence, he gave the new team a familiar name. The original Cincinnati Bengals played in an earlier American Football League (AFL) from 1937 until 1942. Those Bengals were actually the third professional football team to call Cincinnati home. First came the Celts in 1921, followed by the Reds in 1933 and 1934. The first Bengals team lasted longer and drew larger crowds than its predecessors but played in a financially troubled league that went bankrupt after the 1937 season. The AFL reinvented itself in 1939 (and again in 1940), but by 1942, as the United States was entering World War II, the league and the Bengals were done for good. When Brown announced the formation of a new Cincinnati franchise, fans suggested hundreds of possibilities for its name—including Buckeyes, the name of Ohio State University's team. Brown, however, already had a name in mind. It would be Bengals, he said, "to give it a link with past professional football in Cincinnati."

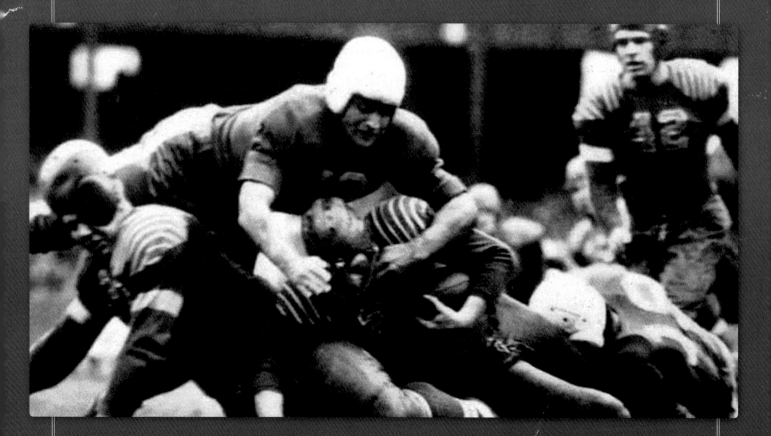

HALFBACK JOHN KOPROWSKI (#23) OF THE ORIGINAL CINCINNATI BENGALS PLAYING IN 1941

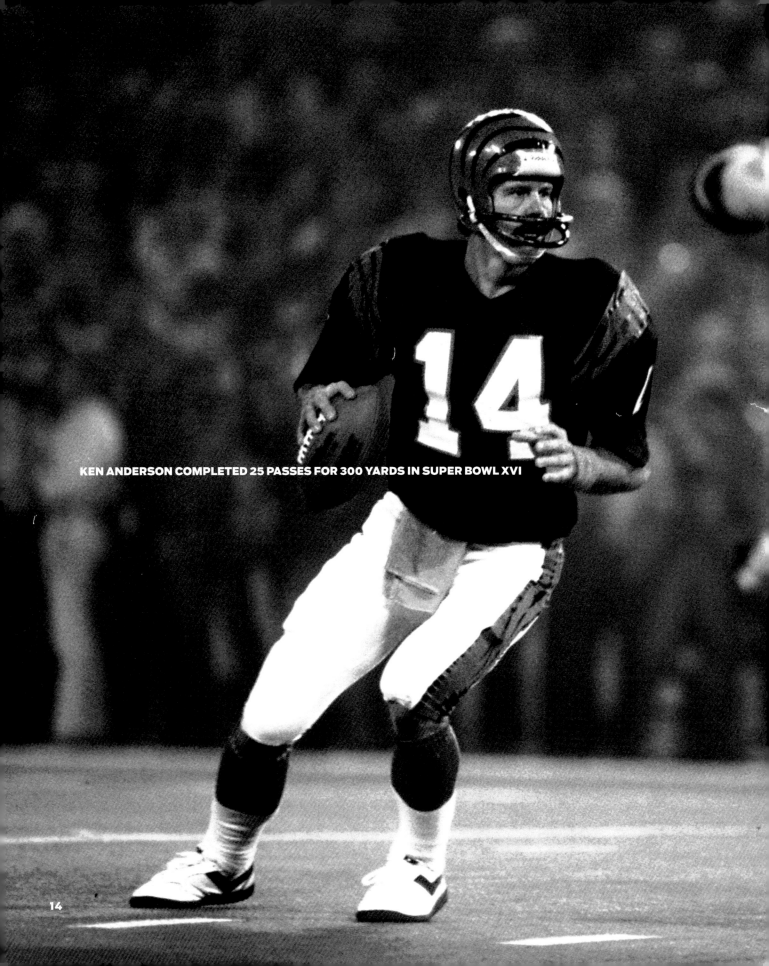

KEN ANDERSON COMPLETED 25 PASSES FOR 300 YARDS IN SUPER BOWL XVI

at the end of the season and was replaced by Sam Wyche, who had been a backup quarterback on the Bengals' roster from 1968 to 1970. His first job was to groom the successor for Anderson: a rookie named Boomer Esiason, who had been picked in the second round of the 1984 NFL Draft.

Esiason had a cannon for an arm and a healthy dose of confidence to match. After injuries sidelined both Anderson and backup Turk Schonert midway through the 1984 season, Esiason eagerly accepted the opportunity to start. "I don't expect to throw five touchdown passes," he told reporters before his first game, "but I also don't expect to throw five interceptions."

Ken Anderson

QUARTERBACK / BENGALS SEASONS: 1971–86 / HEIGHT: 6-FOOT-2 / WEIGHT: 212 POUNDS

Ken Anderson played in one Super Bowl and four Pro Bowls, but it may be his performance in a 1975 *Monday Night Football* game that Cincinnati fans remember best. Anderson, who earned the starting job in 1972, steadily improved under the instruction of renowned quarterbacks coach Bill Walsh. When the team took the field that Monday night in 1975, Anderson threw for what was at the time a franchise-record 447 yards in the Bengals' 33–24 win over the Buffalo Bills. In 1981, Anderson started the season with three interceptions in the first half of the first game—and almost lost his starting position to the third-string quarterback. But he rebounded to throw for 3,754 total yards and 29 touchdowns as he led the Bengals to the Super Bowl that season. "You judge people by how they get up after getting knocked down," said former Bengals offensive lineman Dave Lapham, "and he got up and was league MVP [Most Valuable Player]." Anderson retired as a player in 1986 but returned to Cincinnati as a coach from 1993 through 2002. From 2007 through 2009, he was the quarterbacks coach for the Pittsburgh Steelers.

The No-Huddle Offense

In 1984, Bengals coach Sam Wyche watched his team huddle up on the field to plan in a third-down situation. While his players circled to discuss the play they were going to run, the opposing defense had time to switch out big, slow linebackers for speedier backs who could better cover a deep pass. As Wyche watched that happen, he realized that huddling gave the defense an advantage over the offense. So he started experimenting with what is now known as a no-huddle offense. His players came to the sidelines during timeouts to discuss upcoming plays, then sprinted to the line of scrimmage as soon as the referee blew the whistle. Sometimes, they held a short-and-sweet, five-second "sugar huddle" that didn't give the opposition enough time to prepare for the upcoming play. Throughout the season, they tried several variations, and in 1986, they ended up winning 10 games for the first time in 5 years. Although other teams were slow to adopt it, the Buffalo Bills implemented the no-huddle offense with great success during the 1990s, and other teams have since experimented with it as well.

SAM WYCHE LED THE BENGALS TO THEIR SECOND SUPER BOWL APPEARANCE

Shuffling to the Super Bowl

Esiason took over as the full-time starting quarterback in 1985 and quickly made an impression. He threw for 3,443 yards and 27 touchdowns that season—but he had help. Esiason was protected by an offensive line anchored by Anthony Muñoz, a mountain of a man who was quick, strong, and smart. Balancing Esiason's aerial strikes was the ground game of James Brooks, who rushed for more than 1,000 yards in 1986. The Bengals' 10–6 record that year was an improvement, but it wasn't good enough to take the team back to the playoffs.

Another strike in 1987 slowed Cincinnati's momentum. The highlight of its shortened season was kicker Jim Breech's 97 points scored—tops in the league. Both Breech and Muñoz were key parts of the team's turnaround in 1988. So was a reenergized Esiason, who passed for a total of 3,572 yards and 28 touchdowns.

THE BENGALS CAME UP SHORT IN BOTH SUPER BOWL CLASHES WITH THE 49ERS

Boomer Esiason

QUARTERBACK / BENGALS SEASONS: 1984–92, 1997 / HEIGHT: 6-FOOT-5 / WEIGHT: 224 POUNDS

Norman Julius "Boomer" Esiason's first start as a Bengals player came on a rainy Sunday in October 1984. Although he led Cincinnati to a 13–3 victory over the Houston Oilers that day, the fans didn't get to see any of the gunslinging moves that had defined his college career at the University of Maryland and that would become a hallmark of his professional play. Esiason would go on to toss 247 touchdown passes during his 14-year career, but the only touchdown he scored in that first game was on a quarterback sneak near the muddy goal line. One year later, Esiason replaced longtime fan favorite Ken Anderson under center. Esiason was surprisingly mobile and rushed for almost 1,600 yards during his career. It was his powerful arm, however, that propelled the Bengals to their second Super Bowl appearance, a 20–16 loss to the San Francisco 49ers, in 1988. He left the team five years later to play with the New York Jets and then the Arizona Cardinals, but Esiason returned to Cincinnati to finish his professional playing career with the Bengals in 1997.

"It's a dream come true."

Perhaps the most important factor in the team's 12-win season was rookie running back Elbert "Ickey" Woods, who led Cincinnati with 1,066 rushing yards and scored 15 touchdowns. After making it to the end zone, he entertained fans with a celebratory dance called the "Ickey Shuffle."

Woods and his teammates danced their way through the playoffs, celebrating first a 21–13 victory over the Seattle Seahawks and then a 21–10 win against the Buffalo Bills in the AFC Championship Game. All that remained was Super Bowl XXIII, where the Bengals would once again meet the 49ers. "It's a dream come true," Woods said as the big game approached. "I'm just waiting to score and win the Super Bowl."

But there would be no dancing for Woods and no win for the Bengals in the Super Bowl. The Bengals' offense struggled to move the ball down the field, and the defense suffered a crushing setback when tackle Tim Krumrie's leg was broken during the first quarter. Although the Bengals rebounded in the second half to briefly take the lead, 49ers quarterback Joe Montana broke their hearts by throwing a game-winning touchdown pass with 34 seconds remaining. "It's very disappointing," Esiason said as San Francisco celebrated its 20–16 win. "We were 34 seconds away from a great victory."

Injuries plagued the Bengals the following season. Although Krumrie made an amazing recovery, he wasn't as dominant as he once had been. Woods tore a ligament in his knee in Week 2 and was sidelined for the rest of the season. Esiason struggled with a sore shoulder. Brooks tallied a career-best 1,239 yards, but the 1989 season ended with the Bengals at 8–8 and out of the playoff picture.

Cincinnati's 9–7 record in 1990 earned it a return trip to the playoffs, where the Bengals crushed the Houston Oilers 41–14 in the first round. But the Los Angeles Raiders ended Cincinnati's run a week later, 20–10. Worse yet, team founder and owner Paul Brown died during the off-season. The deflated Bengals struggled through a miserable 3–13 season in 1991.

In 1992, the Bengals hired 32-year-old Dave Shula as their new head coach. Although he was the youngest coach in the NFL, Shula inherited an aging team. His plan for a turnaround involved bringing in young players such as wide receiver Carl Pickens. "I'm hoping to bring a new energy to this franchise," said Shula, the son of legendary Miami Dolphins coach Don Shula. "We've got a long way to go, but we're starting today."

Bengals versus Browns

It was only natural that a rivalry would spring up between the Cincinnati Bengals and the Cleveland Browns. For one, both teams are based in Ohio and are not even 250 miles apart. Both teams' players wear the same shade of orange on their uniforms. Both teams have ties to Paul Brown, who founded and coached both. And because they play in the same division—the AFC North—they play each other regularly enough to keep the rivalry going. Although the Bengals led the all-time series 46–39 through 2015, the balance has swung over the years as each team has gone through good and bad periods. Cincinnati wide receiver Cris Collinsworth remembered how important beating the Browns was in 1981, when the Bengals clinched a division title with a 41–21 win at Cleveland Municipal Stadium. "For Paul Brown, that was something special," Collinsworth said. "Every time we went back to Cleveland, he would have never said it publicly, but you knew it meant a little something more to him."

THE CINCINNATI—CLEVELAND RIVALRY HAS LONG BEEN ONE OF THE NFL'S BEST

GARRISON HEARST WAS ONE OF MANY BENGALS RUSHERS IN THE '90s

Despite the new additions and the contributions of such veterans as running back Harold Green, who rushed for 1,170 yards in 1992, the Bengals fell into the AFC cellar. Muñoz retired in 1992, and Esiason was traded away in 1993, leaving an inexperienced team that lost its first 10 games in 1993 and finished with only 3 wins. That unfortunate scenario played itself out again in 1994, when young quarterback Jeff Blake joined the squad.

Cincinnati badly needed a reversal of fortune. The team hoped that its choice of running back Ki-Jana Carter—a former college star from Penn State University—in the 1995 NFL Draft would provide the spark its offense was lacking. But before the regular season even began, Carter blew out a ligament in his knee and missed all of the 1995 season. Still, Blake gained confidence under center and compiled the stats to prove it. His 3,822 passing yards and 28 touchdowns helped the Bengals improve to 7–9 and earned the young quarterback a trip to the Pro Bowl.

Despite Blake's efforts and the fancy footwork of running back Garrison Hearst, the Bengals continued to lose, and Coach Shula was fired after the Bengals won just one of their first seven games in 1996. Shula, who had compiled a disastrous 19–52 record during slightly more than four years with the team, left football entirely to work in his family's chain of steakhouse restaurants. Owner Mike Brown, who had taken over after his father Paul's death, brought back Bruce Coslet, a former Cincinnati tight end and offensive coordinator, to lead the team. Under Coslet, the Bengals won seven of their last nine games and finished the 1996 season at an even 8–8.

The Who Dey Story

Cincinnati legend has it that the now familiar "Who Dey" chant—which begins with the question, "Who dey think gonna beat dem Bengals?" and is followed by "Noooooboooody"—started during the 1981 season. The Bengals were on a roll, and their happy fans were rolling right along with them. The origins of the chant are unclear. Some credit a local brewer called Hudepohl, whose vendors apparently walked the stadium calling out "Hudey!" instead of "Beer here!"; others say it was stolen from a commercial jingle for a Cincinnati-based auto dealership. However it started, the silly slogan stuck around that whole Super Bowl season and was even recorded as a song by a local television weathercaster. By the time the Bengals returned to the Super Bowl in 1988, the chant had gained national recognition. The Who Dey chant is still proudly hollered at Paul Brown Stadium today and is often started by the Bengals' mascot, a smiling tiger in a football jersey whose name just happens to be Who Dey.

FANS CELEBRATE THE "WHO DEY" STORY WITH BOTH SIGNS AND CHANTS

JEFF BLAKE NEVER BECAME THE BIG STAR THAT SCOUTS HAD PREDICTED

Earning their Stripes

Coslet wasn't the only familiar face on the Bengals' sidelines in 1997. Former quarterback Ken Anderson had returned as the offensive coordinator, and one-time tackle Tim Krumrie was coaching the defensive line. Even Boomer Esiason came back to finish his playing career in Cincinnati, this time as a backup and mentor to Blake.

"There's no hidden agenda or motive on my side," Esiason said. "Jeff is going to let me retire to greener pastures without having to take hits."

But neither Blake nor Esiason, who ended up starting the last five games of the season, would be the star of the show in 1997. Instead, it was rookie running back Corey Dillon who shone brightest, amassing 1,129 rushing yards and scoring 10 touchdowns for an otherwise lackluster offense. Dillon was equally impressive in 1998, but again the rest of the offense, this time led by quarterback Neil O'Donnell, fell flat. By season's end, the Bengals were saddled with another losing record.

After watching the Bengals struggle to find the right fit at quarterback, fans had high

COREY DILLON OFTEN SINGLE-HANDEDLY CARRIED THE BENGALS' OFFENSE

Anthony Muñoz

OFFENSIVE TACKLE / BENGALS SEASONS: 1980–92 / HEIGHT: 6-FOOT-6 / WEIGHT: 280 POUNDS

Both local and national sportswriters thought the Bengals were taking a huge risk when they selected offensive tackle Anthony Muñoz with the third overall pick in the 1980 NFL Draft. The mountainous Muñoz had spent much of his final two seasons at the University of Southern California sidelined by knee problems. But the Bengals took a chance on the two-time All-American—and they were roundly rewarded. Muñoz joined the offensive line as a left tackle during his rookie year and was an anchor there for 13 straight seasons. His sheer physical presence gave him an advantage in blocking opposing defenders, but his quick feet and sure hands made him a solid receiver as well—he nabbed seven catches and scored four touchdowns during his Hall of Fame career. Muñoz went to the Pro Bowl 11 times and played in 2 Super Bowls, both against the San Francisco 49ers. He retired in 1992 and was inducted into the Pro Football Hall of Fame in 1998. Afterward, Muñoz continued to live near Cincinnati and helped broadcast some of the Bengals' preseason games on a local television station.

hopes for the nimble Akili Smith, who had been chosen with the third overall pick in the 1999 NFL Draft. But Smith was benched after struggling as a starter in 1999 and never lived up to the expectations the team had for him. The only bright spots in the disappointing 4–12 season were Dillon's hard charging and kick returner Tremain Mack's club-record average of 27.1 yards per return. As Cincinnati ended the 1990s with a disgraceful 52–108 combined record, the national media began referring to the team as "The Bungles."

On September 10, 2000, more than 64,000 fans gathered to watch those "Bungles" play their first game in the state-of-the-art Paul Brown Stadium. After a dismal decade, both the team and its fans were hoping that a new home might reinvigorate the sagging franchise. But when the Bengals fell to the Browns 24–7 that day and were shut out in the next two games as well, it became obvious that Cincinnati needed more than a simple change of scenery to regain its winning ways.

Even though the Bengals finished 4–12, there were signs of improvement during the 2000 season. Slick young receiver Peter Warrick, who scored the second Bengals touchdown in Paul Brown Stadium, showed signs of stardom, and Dillon ran his way into the NFL record books with a 278-yard performance in October, breaking Chicago Bears great Walter Payton's record for a single-game rushing total. The Pro

Football Hall of Fame honored the hard-charging halfback by displaying the jersey, pants, and cleats he wore that day. "Not many athletes get the opportunity to get their uniform inducted into the Hall of Fame," Dillon commented.

But even as individuals were becoming stars, the team as a whole was struggling to merely come close to a winning record. Veteran Jon Kitna took over for Akili Smith at quarterback in 2001. Helped by a strong, young defense anchored by end Vaughn Booker and linebacker Takeo Spikes, Kitna managed to guide the team to an improved 6–10 record. However, the following year, after recruiting veteran Gus Frerotte as the fifth quarterback to play under center in 5 seasons, the team set a new low, earning just 2 wins and 14 losses.

JON KITNA'S TOUGHNESS AND SMARTS WON OVER FANS IN CINCINNATI

The Ickey Shuffle

As the 1988 Bengals marched toward the Super Bowl, an unexpected star shuffled along with them: rookie running back Elbert "Ickey" Woods, who scored 15 touchdowns during the course of the season. As much as the fans appreciated those points, what they really loved was the dance Woods did in the end zone each time. After each touchdown, he would face the crowds with his arms stretched out wide, then hop twice to the left, twice to the right, spike the ball, and, finally, twirl his right index finger over his head while swiveling his hips and shouting, "Woo! Woo! Woo!" His silly dance was dubbed the "Ickey Shuffle" by the local media, and it was soon being duplicated by teammates, fans, and even team owner Paul Brown, who was 80 years old at the time. Woods's dance sparked Ickey songs, shirts, commercials, and even an Ickey milk shake. More important to Woods, however, was that he was celebrating Cincinnati victories. "I got to do it 15 times that year," he said. "I was in the right place at the right time."

ICKEY WOODS EARNED RENOWN AS AN END ZONE CELEBRATION PIONEER

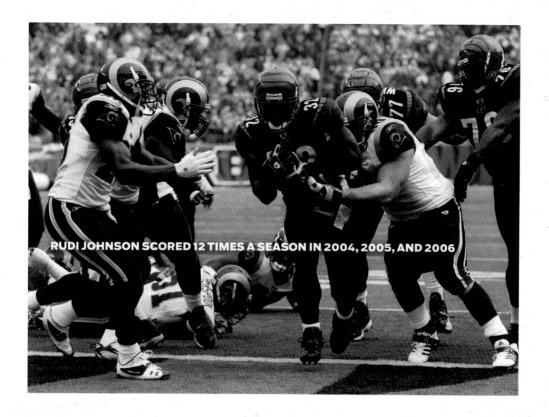

RUDI JOHNSON SCORED 12 TIMES A SEASON IN 2004, 2005, AND 2006

By the beginning of the 2003 season, new coach Marvin Lewis had reworked the roster so that more than half the players were new to the team—including Carson Palmer, a strong-armed quarterback taken with the first overall pick in the 2003 NFL Draft. Although Palmer would spend his first season learning from Kitna, his development as the quarterback of the future was part of Lewis's long-term plan for the Bengals' improvement.

While Palmer watched from the sidelines, Kitna had a sensational year, connecting with flashy receiver Chad Johnson (who later changed his name to Chad Ochocinco) for 1,355 of his total 3,591 passing yards. After an injury slowed Dillon, Rudi Johnson came off the bench to tally almost 1,000 yards and score 9 touchdowns. Bengals fans were so charmed by the unassuming young running back that they began cheering "Roo-dee! Roo-dee!" every time he touched the ball. After losing the first three games of the season, the Bengals made a remarkable recovery to finish 8–8 and out of the cellar in the AFC North (which they had joined in 2002). "It was a good year," Coach Lewis said. "Not a great year—a good year."

In 2004, Palmer was ready to prove that he could take over as quarterback. He threw for 2,897 yards and 18 touchdowns, Rudi Johnson ran for more than 1,000 yards, and cornerback Tory James snagged 8 interceptions—all of which helped Cincinnati repeat the success of 2003 with another 8–8 record and third place in the division. Although the Bengals were again left out of the playoffs, Cincinnati fans celebrated their success all season long with record-setting attendance at Paul Brown Stadium. Each of the eight regular-season home games sold out for the first time since 1992.

CARSON PALMER EMERGED AS A STAR IN 2005, REENERGIZING THE BENGALS FAITHFUL

CHAD JOHNSON WAS BRASH BUT ALWAYS DELIVERED MAXIMUM EFFORT

Roaring Back

In 2005, the Bengals were finally able to reward the loyalty of their fans. Cincinnati roared out of the starting blocks with four consecutive wins and ended the season with the division title and an 11–5 record. Palmer led the league with 32 touchdown passes, thanks in part to an impenetrable offensive line that set a team record by allowing only 21 quarterback sacks all season. The defense, meanwhile, helped out by making 31 interceptions—including 10 by cornerback Deltha O'Neal.

For the first time in 15 years, the Bengals were participating in the playoffs, and Cincinnati eagerly prepared to host the Pittsburgh Steelers in the AFC Wild Card game. Palmer's first pass of the game sailed 66 yards downfield before landing gently in the arms of an open receiver—but back at the line of scrimmage, the young quarterback was on the ground, writhing in pain after being hit just as the ball had left his hand. As Palmer was carried off the field with a badly injured knee, backup quarterback Kitna tried to save the game. Although Kitna led the Bengals to a 17–14 lead at halftime,

DELTHA O'NEAL PROVED STICKY-FINGERED, MAKING 34 CAREER INTERCEPTIONS

✕Tim Krumrie

NOSE TACKLE / BENGALS SEASONS: 1983–94 / HEIGHT: 6-FOOT-2 / WEIGHT: 270 POUNDS

Tim Krumrie may be best remembered for the sickening sight of his left leg being shattered before a television audience of millions as the Bengals battled the San Francisco 49ers in Super Bowl XXIII in January 1989. But Krumrie, who played six more seasons in Cincinnati, is known as one of the best defensive linemen ever to play for the Bengals because of the hits he made—not the hits he took. The Wisconsin native, who grew up on a dairy farm, was known by teammates and opponents alike for his toughness and intensity and quickly established himself as a legend on the defensive line. During his 12-year career with the Bengals, the hulking Krumrie made 1,008 tackles and 34.5 sacks and recovered 13 fumbles. He played in two Pro Bowls; his second appearance, in 1988, was the last time a Bengals defensive lineman had received such recognition until Geno Atkins was invited to the Pro Bowl in 2012. Krumrie retired in 1994, having played his entire career in Cincinnati, and went on to coach for the Bengals and to serve as a defensive line coach for the Kansas City Chiefs until 2010.

the Steelers scored 17 unanswered points in the second half to win, 31–17.

Although some experts thought that Palmer's knee injury would end his career, the young quarterback made an amazing comeback. Not only did he start every game of the 2006 season, but he also set a new team record with 4,035 passing yards. T. J. Houshmandzadeh and Chad Johnson each recorded more than 1,000 receiving yards, while O'Neal spearheaded the defense. Going into the final game of the season against the Steelers, the Bengals had a shot at claiming the Wild Card spot in the playoffs. But their hopes of returning to the postseason were dashed when the Steelers pulled off a 23–17 overtime victory.

When the Bengals started the 2007 season with a 27–20 win over the Baltimore Ravens, the playoffs again seemed within reach. But then Cincinnati lost its next

ANTONIO CHATMAN RETURNED KICKS FOR CINCINNATI IN THE LATE 2000s

four games and dropped to a disappointing 7–9 record, well out of contention for postseason play. Palmer was sidelined for most of the 2008 season with an elbow injury, leaving the Bengals to muddle through with only four wins.

Palmer's first game back in 2009 was a loss against the Denver Broncos in the season opener. But then the Bengals went on a tear, winning seven of their next eight games and sweeping all six games against AFC North opponents. With an impressive 10–6 record, Cincinnati found itself atop the division and back in the playoffs again as well. This time, the Bengals faced the New York Jets in the first round. Cincinnati took an early lead with a first-quarter touchdown, but then sloppy play—including a Palmer interception and two missed field goals—let the Jets come back and win it, 24–14.

Although that loss put Cincinnati in the NFL record books for enduring the most consecutive years—19—without a playoff win, it didn't diminish the Bengals' hopes for the 2010 season. Fans were

A Tale of Two Stadiums

For nearly 30 years, the Cincinnati Bengals shared Riverfront Stadium (which became known as Cinergy Field in 1996) with the Cincinnati Reds baseball team. But in 2000, the Bengals got a brand-new, state-of-the-art stadium of their own: Paul Brown Stadium, named after the man who had started the team and served as its head coach through 1975. Although the Bengals had sold naming rights for their previous home to Cinergy, an electric utility company, for $6 million, team president Mike Brown wasn't interested in doing the same for the new stadium. He insisted that it bear the name of his father. "We like that our stadium name honors the tradition of the NFL," Brown said. "Many names now don't have anything to do with the game." Cinergy Field, meanwhile, was destroyed. In December 2002, the statuesque old structure came down, imploded section by section with the help of more than 1,200 pounds of dynamite and nitroglycerin. The United Way charity held a raffle to pick one person to push the ceremonial button to bring the building down and raised more than $20,000 in the process.

PAUL BROWN STADIUM IS OFTEN CALLED "THE JUNGLE" BY BENGALS FANS

THE BENGALS IN ACTION AGAINST THE DIVISIONAL OPPONENT BALTIMORE RAVENS

43

ANDREW HAWKINS WAS SMALL (5-FOOT-7 AND 175 POUNDS) BUT ELUSIVE

especially excited when electrifying wide receiver Terrell Owens joined the team on the first day of training camp. At the time, Owens was third all-time among NFL receivers for total yardage, and his addition seemed to give the offense another powerful weapon. But even Owens couldn't help Cincinnati break out of a 10-game losing streak in 2010. With just four wins, the Bengals plunged back to the bottom of the AFC North.

O wens, who had agreed to just a one-year contract with Cincinnati, was gone at the end of that dismal season. So was Palmer, who had asked team ownership to trade him and opted to retire when his request was refused. When rookie quarterback Andy Dalton helped the Bengals win four of their first six games in 2010, however, Bengals owner Mike Brown relented and sent Palmer to the Oakland Raiders in exchange for a pair of draft picks. Dalton, Brown said, "has shown himself to be one of the best and most exciting young quarterbacks in the NFL."

Dalton led a roster crowded with young players—including fellow rookies A. J. Green and Andrew Hawkins, both wide receivers, and defensive tackle Geno Atkins—back into playoff contention in 2011. With veterans such as running back Cedric Benson and defensive end Robert Geathers helping those youngsters develop, the Bengals finished at 9–7, in third place in the AFC North and in the perfect position to fill a Wild Card slot in the playoffs. Cincinnati lost to the Houston Texans in the first round, but the team's improved performance gave fans a reason to look forward to the 2012 season.

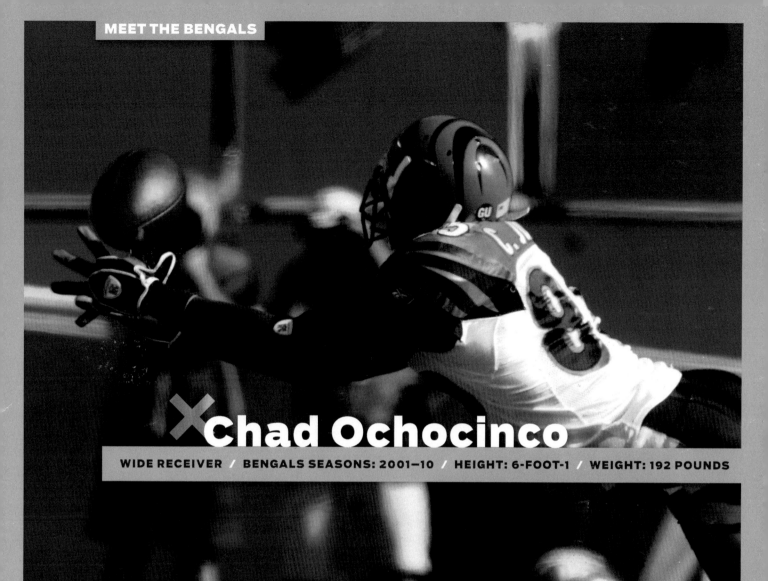

✕ Chad Ochocinco

WIDE RECEIVER / BENGALS SEASONS: 2001–10 / HEIGHT: 6-FOOT-1 / WEIGHT: 192 POUNDS

Chad Ochocinco began his football career as Chad Johnson, a speedy and sure-handed receiver at Oregon State University. But after becoming known as one of the best—and most flamboyant—receivers in the NFL as number 85 for the Cincinnati Bengals, he legally changed his last name from Johnson to Ochocinco, which is Spanish for "eight five," before the 2008 season. Even before changing his name, Ochocinco had gained almost as much notoriety for his behavior off the field as he had for his record-setting performances on it (he held the team records for most receiving yards all-time and in a season). He had a love-hate relationship with the media, refusing to speak with reporters at times and then using interviews to complain about his teammates and coaches or to boast about his achievements when he wanted to. Ochocinco so enjoyed the spotlight that he sought it outside the football arena as well. Among his many off-season activities were appearing as a celebrity contestant on the TV show *Dancing with the Stars* and serving as a guest wrestling host on an episode of *WWE Monday Night Raw*.

ANDY DALTON SHOWED TERRIFIC LEADERSHIP SKILLS EVEN AS AN NFL ROOKIE

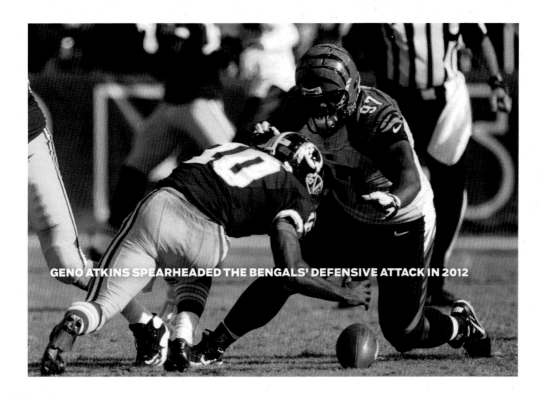

GENO ATKINS SPEARHEADED THE BENGALS' DEFENSIVE ATTACK IN 2012

In 2012, the Bengals improved to first place in the AFC North—tied at season's end with the eventual Super Bowl champion Ravens. Running back BenJarvus Green-Ellis, nicknamed "The Law Firm," helped Cincinnati's cause in his first season with the team, rushing for more than 1,000 yards. Meanwhile, Green proved his rock-solid reliability in his sophomore effort, his 97 receptions ranking 7th-best in the league. "When something needs to be done or a play needs to be made, he's the guy people look up to," said rookie wide receiver Marvin Jones of Green. "That's the kind of guy you want around you." Green and Dalton spearheaded a return to the playoffs, but the Bengals lost to the Houston Texans in the first round—their fifth straight playoff loss since 1991.

The Bengals continued to dominate the AFC North, finishing first or second in the division for the next three years. Cincinnati also made the playoffs every year but struggled to get past the first round. After being knocked out of the playoffs five years in a row, the Bengals set a less-than-desirable NFL record for most consecutive opening-round losses.

Although the Bengals have had their share of subpar seasons, they've also continually given Cinicinnati's fans reason to keep hoping for better years to come. Those fans know that their team is far from the "Bungles" they were once known as and that, someday soon, they will be better known as Super Bowl champions instead.